Sign & Say

36 Bible Verses for Children

Daphna Flegal

ISBN: 9781426744419

PACP01023006-01

Editor: Daphna Flegal
Production Editor: David Whitworth
Designer: Kent Sneed and Kellie Green
Art: Diana Magnuson

12 13 14 15 16 17 18 19 20 21—10 9 8 7 6 5 4 3 2 1

Printed in the U. S. A.

Contents

Old Testament

New Testament

Sign and Say

Introduction

Why teach Bible verses using signs from American Sign Language? Because children learn in a variety of ways.

Some children prefer to learn through listening and talking. Using signs from American Sign Language (ASL) appeals to these children because it introduces them to another language. Other children prefer to learn through movement. Using ASL signs naturally appeals to these children. The child who prefers to learn visually will appreciate watching how the signs are made. The child who loves being involved in a group activity will enjoy learning the signs as a group. The child who is a logical learner will appreciate the step-by-step instructions for signing. The benefit of teaching Bible verses with signs from American Sign Language is that it allows children to learn through seeing, hearing, and movement. This multiple stimulation creates more pathways in the brain. The more pathways in the brain, the stronger the memory. This means that children remember more easily what they learn when you involve both their bodies and their minds—and we want them to remember Bible verses.

Sign and Say: 36 Bible Verses for Children will help your children learn Bible verses using the hand motions of American Sign Language. The verses are not actually translated into American Sign Language. ASL, like any other language, has its own syntax, the rules for making phrases and sentences. Instead, each Bible verse is presented along with the signs for key words in the verse. Use the simple steps listed below to learn these verses yourself and then teach the verses to your children.

- Look at the illustrations.
- Read the written directions.
- Practice, practice, practice! *(You need to be able to sign the verse for the children without looking at the page.)*

Demonstration videos are available at AbingdonPress.com/downloads.

A special word of thanks to Diana Rose Flegal and Leigh Ann Scott for their help with *Sign and Say: 36 Bible Verses for Children.*

Diana, my daughter, is fluent in American Sign Language and holds an MS in Teacher Education, Education of the Deaf and Hard of Hearing from the University of Tennessee. She has taught Deaf students in Alabama and Tennessee Public Schools for the past seven years. She also teaches Sign Language Club at a local middle school and interprets extracurricular events for students.

Leigh Ann is Lead Advertising Copywriter at The United Methodist Publishing House. She has interpreted in office settings for colleagues who are deaf, and has demonstrated sign language in video segments for Cokesbury children's curriculum and VBS resources. She has has also interpreted worship services and classes at two local congregations.

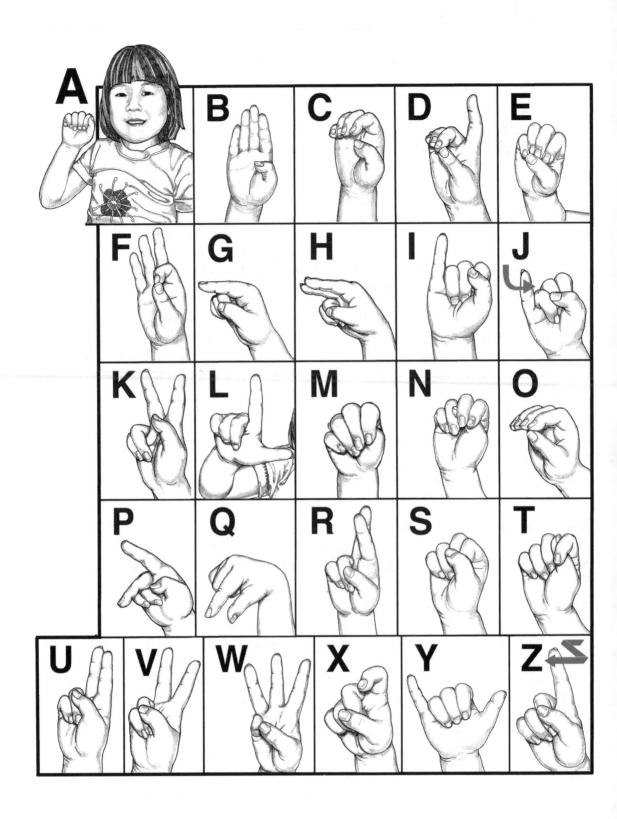

Genesis 1:31

God saw everything he had made: it was supremely good.

God
Point the index finger of your right hand, with the other fingers curled down. Bring the hand down in front of your face as if you are drawing a shepherd's crook. Open the palm as you bring your hand down. End with your hand flat and your palm facing left.

Saw
Hold your fingers in a V-shape. Touch the V beneath one eye. Move the hand forward.

Everything (All)
Hold the left palm toward the body. Circle the right hand out and around the left palm. End with the back of the right hand in the open left hand.

God
Point the index finger of your right hand, with the other fingers curled down. Bring the hand down in front of your face as if you are drawing a shepherd's crook. Open the palm as you bring your hand down. End with your hand flat and your palm facing left.

Made
Make fists with both hands. Place the right fist on the left fist. Twist the fists from side to side in opposite directions and tap them together.

Good
Touch the fingers of your right hand to your chin, Move the hand forward and drop it the back of the hand into the open palm of the left hand.

Sign and Say    7

God said, "I'll be with you."

God
Point the index finger of your right hand, with the other fingers curled down. Bring the hand down in front of your face as if you are drawing a shepherd's crook. Open the palm as you bring your hand down. End with your hand flat and your palm facing left.

Said
Point your index finger at your chin several times.

I (Me)
Point to yourself.

With
Make fists with both hands, with the thumbs out. Place the fists together, with curled fingers touching.

You
Point out with your index finger.

Sign and Say

Honor your father and your mother.

Honor
Hold up the first two fingers on each hand. Place one hand slightly below the other. Bring both hands together in an arch away from your face and down.

Father
Hold your right hand with fingers and thumb spread out as you would to show the number five. Touch the tip of your thumb to your forehead.

Mother
Hold your right hand with fingers and thumb spread out as you would to show the number five. Touch the tip of your thumb to your chin and wiggle your fingers slightly.

Joshua 24:24

We will serve the LORD our God and will obey him.

Serve
Hold both hands palms up. Move your hands several times in front of your body with one hand moving forward while the other hand moves backward.

Lord
Make an "L" with the right index finger and thumb. Place the "L" at the left shoulder and then move the "L" across the body to the right waist.

Obey
Hold both hands with thumb and fingertips closed together at eye level with palms facing your body. Drop both hands down and open the fists with the palms facing up.

   Sign and Say

The LORD sees into the heart.

Lord
Make an "L" with the right index finger and thumb. Place the "L" at the left shoulder and then move the "L" across the body to the right waist.

Sees
Hold your fingers in a V-shape. Touch the V beneath one eye. Move the hand forward.

Heart
Use the second finger on each hand to outline the shape of a heart over the position of your actual heart.

LORD, our Lord, how majestic is your name throughout the earth!

Lord
Make an "L" with the right index finger and thumb. Place the "L" at the left shoulder and then move the "L" across the body to the right waist.

Majestic (Great)
Raise both hands up head high with palms facing out. Push hands forward and up.

Majestic *continued*
Then bring hands down to shoulder level and push hands slightly forward and up again.

Name
Extend the first two fingers of both hands. Cross the fingers of the right hand over the fingers of the left hand, forming an X. Tap the fingers together several times.

Earth
Place your right thumb and right middle finger on the back of the left hand near the wrist and rock the right hand back and forth.

Sign and Say

You, LORD, are all I want! You are my choice.

You
Point out with your index finger.

Lord
Make an "L" with the right index finger and thumb. Place the "L" at the left shoulder and then move the "L" across the body to the right waist.

All
Hold the left palm toward the body. Circle the right hand out and around the left palm. End with the back of the right hand in the open left hand.

I (Me)
Point to yourself.

Want
Hold out both hands with palms up and fingers slightly curved. Move both hands toward your body with your fingers curling in.

Choice
Make a "V" with the first two fingers of your left hand. Move the thumb and index finger of your right hand as if you are picking something off each finger of the "V."

Psalm 23:1

The LORD is my shepherd.

Lord
Make an "L" with the right index finger and thumb. Place the "L" at the left shoulder and then move the "L" across the body to the right waist.

Shepherd
Hold your left fist out, palm down. Place your right hand on the left arm and make a cutting motion with the first two fingers.

Shepherd *continued*
Hold hands open, with palms facing each other in front of your body. Move both hands down in a parallel motion.

Sign and Say

Hope in the LORD! Be strong! Let your heart take courage! Hope in the LORD!

Hope
Hold both hands with your palms open, facing the sides of your head. Your right hand should be above your head. Your left hand should be at eye level. Moving both hands at the same time, bend your hands to make a right angle with your fingers and then unbend them so that the fingers point straight up.

Lord
Make an "L" with the right index finger and thumb. Place the "L" at the left shoulder and then move the "L" across the body to the right waist.

Strong (Courage)
Hold both hands with your palms facing your shoulders and your fingers spread apart. Bring both hands forward as you close both hands into fists with the thumbs on the outside.

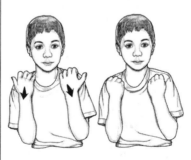

Heart
Use the second finger on each hand to outline the shape of a heart over the position of your actual heart.

Courage
Hold both hands with your palms facing your shoulders and your fingers spread apart. Bring both hands forward as you close both hands into fists with the thumbs on the outside.

But I will remember the LORD's deeds; yes, I will remember your wondrous acts from times long past.

Remember
Curl both hands into fists with the thumbs out. Touch the right thumb to your forehead. Bring your right thumb down and place it on top of your left thumb.

Lord's
Make an "L" with the right index finger and thumb. Place the "L" at the left shoulder and then move the "L" across the body to the right waist.

Deeds
Form a "C" with each hand, with palms facing down. Move your hands right and left several times.

Wondrous (Great)
Raise both hands up head high with palms facing out. Push hands forward and up. Then bring hands down to shoulder level and push hands slightly forward and up again.

Acts (Deeds)
Form a "C" with each hand, with palms facing down. Move your hands right and left several times.

Past
Hold your open hand in front of the right shoulder with your palm facing your body. Move the hand backwards over the shoulder.

Sign and Say

Psalm 100:1

Shout triumphantly to the LORD, all the earth!

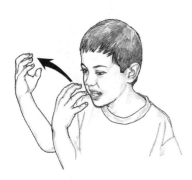

Shout
Cup your right hand in front of your mouth and quickly move the hand up and away from your mouth.

Triumphantly (Celebrate)
Hold both hands above your shoulders with each index finger bent into a crook shape. The remaining fingers are curled into the palms with thumbs on top. Circle your hands up higher.

Lord
Make an "L" with the right index finger and thumb. Place the "L" at the left shoulder and then move the "L" across the body to the right waist.

All
Hold the left palm toward the body. Circle the right hand out and around the left palm. End with the back of the right hand in the open left hand.

Earth
Place your right thumb and right middle finger on the back of the left hand near the wrist and rock the right hand back and forth.

Because the LORD is good, his loyal love lasts forever; his faithfulness lasts generation after generation.

Lord
Make an "L" with the right index finger and thumb. Place the "L" at the left shoulder and then move the "L" across the body to the right waist.

Good
Touch the fingers of your right hand to your chin. Move the hand forward and drop the back of the hand into the open palm of the left hand.

Love
Cross your fists at the wrists and press them to your heart.

Forever
Hold up your right index finger and circle it in the air. Then bring your hand down and out with the thumb and little finger straight out. The three middle fingers are curled into the palm.

Faithfulness
Touch your right index finger to your forehead. Bring down your right hand, touching the tip of your index finger to the tip of your thumb to form a circle. Bring your left hand up with the index finger and thumb forming a second circle. Tap the two circles together.

Generation
Hold both hands in front of your right shoulder with the palms facing your body. Roll your hands down from the shoulder.

Sign and Say

Psalm 118:24

This is the day the LORD acted; we will rejoice and celebrate in it!

Day
Extend the index finger of the right hand. Hold the left arm parallel to the floor. Place the right elbow at the left index finger. Move the right index finger down in an arc until it touches the inside of the left elbow.

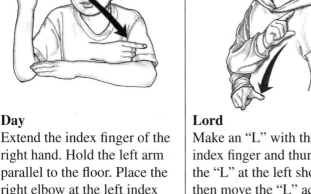

Lord
Make an "L" with the right index finger and thumb. Place the "L" at the left shoulder and then move the "L" across the body to the right waist.

Acted (Made)
Make fists with both hands. Place the right fist on the left fist. Twist the fists from side to side in opposite directions and tap them together.

Celebrate
Hold both hands above your shoulders with each index finger bent into a crook shape. The remaining fingers are curled into the palms with thumbs on top. Circle your hands up higher.

Psalm 122:1

I rejoiced with those who said to me, "Let's go to the LORD's house!"

I (Me)
Point to yourself.

Rejoice (Celebrate)
Hold both hands above your shoulders with each index finger bent into a crook shape. The remaining fingers are curled into the palms with thumbs on top. Circle your hands up higher.

Said
Point your index finger at your chin several times.

Me
Point to yourself.

Go
Point both index fingers away from the body in one quick movement.

Lord's
Make an "L" with the right index finger and thumb. Place the "L" at the left shoulder and then move the "L" across the body to the right waist.

House
Touch the fingertips of both hands together in the shape of a roof. Bring the hands apart and down to outline the walls of the imaginary house.

Sign and Say

Psalm 150:6

Let every living thing praise the LORD! Praise the LORD!

Everything (All)
Hold the left palm toward the body. Circle the right hand out and around the left palm. End with the back of the right hand in the open left hand.

Living
Hold both hands at your waist with your thumbs and index fingers pointing out. Move your hands up and along your chest.

Praise
Bring both hands up and clap your hands several times.

Lord
Make an "L" with the right index finger and thumb. Place the "L" at the left shoulder and then move the "L" across the body to the right waist.

Proverbs 17:17

Friends love all the time.

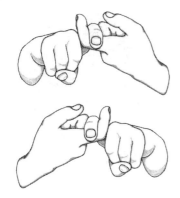

Friends
Hold out both hands with index fingers extended. Hook your right index finger over the left index finger. Reverse.

Love
Cross your fists at the wrists and press them to your heart.

All Time (Forever)
Hold up your right index finger and circle it in the air. Then bring your hand down and out with the thumb and little finger straight out. The three middle fingers are curled into the palm.

22   Sign and Say

A child is born to us.

Child (Baby)
Place your arms like you are holding a baby. Rock.

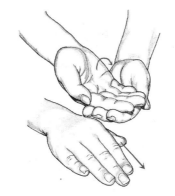

Born
Hold your right hand palm down on your abdomen. Then put the back of the right hand in the palm of the left hand. Slide your right hand under your left hand.

Us
Hold up the first two fingers of your right hand, pressing the other fingers down with the thumb. Touch your right shoulder with this hand. Circle your hand out and touch the fingers to your left shoulder.

And a little child will lead them.

Little
Hold out both hands with palms facing each other and fingers extended. Start with your hands apart and move them closer together.

Child
Pretend to pat the head of a small child.

Lead
Hold your left hand about chest high with your palm flat and fingers together. Grasp your left fingers with your right hand and pull the left hand away from your body.

Sign and Say

Matthew 5:9

Happy are people who make peace, because they will be called God's children.

Happy
Hold both hands with palms open facing the chest and thumbs pointing up. Pat the chest in an upward motion several times.

People
Make the "P" letter sign (see page 6) with both hands. Circle your hands in front of your body.

Make
Make fists with both hands. Place the right fist on the left fist. Twist the fists from side to side in opposite directions and tap them together.

Peace
Place the right palm on top of the left palm. Turn your hands so that the left palm is on top of the right palm. Move both palms down and to the sides.

Called (Named)
Extend the first two fingers of both hands. Cross the fingers of the right hand over the fingers of the left hand, forming an X. Tap the fingers together several times.

God's
Point the index finger of your right hand, with the other fingers curled down. Bring the hand down in front of your face. Open the palm as you bring your hand down.

Children
Move both hands, palms down, as if you are patting the heads of several children.

Bring in your kingdom so that your will is done on earth as it's done in heaven.

Bring
Hold both hands on your right side at waist level, palms up. Move both hands in front of your body over to the left side.

Kingdom
Make a "K" with the right index finger and thumb (see page 6). Place the "K" at the left shoulder and then move the "K" across the body to the right waist.

Kingdom *continued*
Flatten both hands and hold them palms down. Place the left hand near the right hip and move the right hand outward in a circle.

Will
Touch the right palm to your heart. Bring your hand out and slightly down.

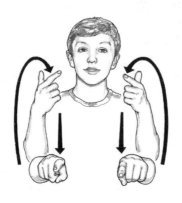

Done (Happens)
Hold both hands in a fist with the index fingers extended and palms facing up. Flip your fists over so that your palms face down.

Earth
Place your right thumb and right middle finger on the back of the left hand near the wrist and rock the right hand back and forth.

Sign and Say

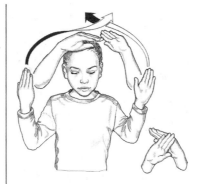

As it's done (Same)
Hold your hand with your thumb and little finger out and your first three fingers curled down. Your palm faces down. Move your hand from side to side.

Heaven
Bend both arms at the elbows and hold both hands with fingers together pointing straight up. Then move both arms together in an arc above your head. Just before the hands touch, move the right hand, palm down, so that it sweeps under the left hand and then up, ending with the palm of the right hand facing out.

Therefore, you should treat people in the same way that you want people to treat you.

Treat (Care for)
Hold both hands in a "C" shape. Place your right "C" on top of your left "C." Make small circles with both hands together.

People
Make the "P" letter sign (see page 6) with both hands. Circle your hands in front of your body.

Same
Hold your hand with your thumb and little finger out and your first three fingers curled down. Your palm faces down. Move your hand from side to side.

You
Point away from yourself.

Want
Hold out both hands with palms up and fingers slightly curved. Move both hands toward your body with your fingers curling in.

People
Make the "P" letter sign (see page 6) with both hands. Circle your hands in front of your body.

Treat (Care for)
Hold both hands in a "C" shape. Place your right "C" on top of your left "C." Make small circles with both hands together.

You
Point away from yourself.

Sign and Say

Allow the children to come to me.

Allow (Permit)
Hold your hands with palms facing each other. Scoop both hands frontwards and up.

Children
Move both hands, palms down, as if you are patting the heads of several children.

Come
Hold out your hand with index finger extended, palm up. Move your hand toward yourself.

Me
Point to yourself.

Mark 8:29

Peter answered, "You are the Christ."

You
Point away from yourself.

Christ
Make a "C" with your right hand. Place the "C" at the left shoulder and then move the "C" across the body to the right waist.

Sign and Say

Mark 11:9

Hosanna! Blessings on the one who comes in the name of the Lord!

Hosanna
Clap your hands and then hold up the first two fingers on each hand. Sweep your hands out as if directing a choir.

Blessings
Touch your thumb and fingers together on both hands. Touch your hands to your mouth. Move both hands down and flatten them with palms down and your fingers spread apart.

One
Hold up your index finger.

Comes
Hold out your hand with index finger extended, palm up. Move your hand toward yourself.

Name
Extend the first two fingers of both hands. Cross the fingers of the right hand over the fingers of the left hand, forming an X. Tap the fingers together several times.

Lord
Make an "L" with the right index finger and thumb. Place the "L" at the left shoulder and then move the "L" across the body to the right waist.

Sign and Say

The angel said, "Don't be afraid! Look! I bring good news to you—wonderful, joyous news for all people."

Angel
Place the fingertips of both hands at the shoulders. Turn hands out as if making wings.

Said
Point your index finger at your chin several times.

Don't (Not)
Hold your hand in a fist with the thumb extended. Touch the thumb to your chin and then move your thumb forward while shaking your head from side to side.

Afraid
Quickly hold up both hands in front of your body with your fingers spread wide as if you are startled.

I (Me)
Point to yourself.

Bring
Hold both hands on your right side at waist level, palms up. Move both hands in front of your body over to the left side.

Sign and Say

Good
Touch the fingers of your right hand to your chin. Move the hand forward and drop the back of the hand into the open palm of the left hand.

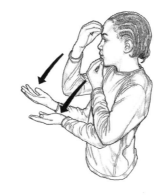

News (Information)
Hold both hands with fingers and thumb closed together near the body. Place one hand higher than the other. Move your hands away form your body and open them with your palms facing up.

For
Touch your index finger to your forehead and then quickly point out.

All
Hold the left palm toward the body. Circle the right hand out and around the left palm. End with the back of the right hand in the open left hand.

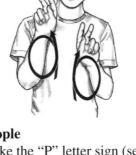

People
Make the "P" letter sign (see page 6) with both hands. Circle your hands in front of your body.

Luke 10:27

You must love the Lord your God with all your heart, with all your being, with all your strength, and with all your mind, and love your neighbor as yourself.

You
Point away from yourself.

Love
Cross your fists at the wrists and press them to your heart.

Lord
Make an "L" with the right index finger and thumb. Place the "L" at the left shoulder and then move the "L" across the body to the right waist.

All
Hold the left palm toward the body. Circle the right hand out and around the left palm. End with the back of the right hand in the open left hand.

Heart
Use the second finger on each hand to outline the shape of a heart over the position of your actual heart.

Being (Body)
Hold your hand flat with fingers together. Pat your chest and then slide your hand to your waist.

Sign and Say

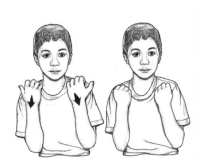

Strength (Courage)
Hold both hands with your palms facing your shoulders and your fingers spread apart. Bring both hands forward as you close both hands into fists with the thumbs on the outside.

Mind
Tap your index finger to your forehead twice.

Neighbor
Hold your hands in loose fists with thumbs pointing up and tap the knuckles together. Open your hands straight in front of you and lower them.

As (Same)
Hold your hand with your thumb and little finger out and your first three fingers curled down. Your palm faces down. Move your hand from side to side.

Yourself
Hold your hand in a fist with your thumb up. Tip your fist forward.

God so loved the world that he gave his only Son, so that everyone who believes in him won't perish but will have eternal life.

God
Point the index finger of your right hand, with the other fingers curled down. Bring the hand down as if drawing a shepherd's crook while opening the palm.

Loved
Cross your fists at the wrists and press them to your heart.

World
Hold out your first three fingers on each hand. Circle your hands around each other in one complete circle. End with one hand on top of the other.

Gave
Hold both hands in front of your body, palms up and fingers and thumb touching on each hand. Move your hands up and away from your chest.

Only
Extend the index finger of your right hand with palm facing out. Twist the hand to the left so that the palm faces the body.

Son
Bring your thumb and extended fingers of your right hand to the right side of your forehead as if you are grasping an imaginary hat brim. Then rest the right hand in the left elbow and swing your arms as if rocking a baby.

Sign and Say

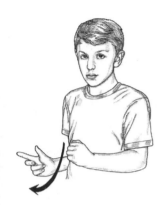

Everyone
Make fists with both hands, with your thumbs out. Hold up the left fist and with the thumb of the right fist, stroke down the left thumb. Then move the right hand out and up with the index finger extended.

Believes
Touch your forehead with the index finger of your right hand. Bring your hand down, palm flat, to meet your left hand, palm up. Clasp your hands together.

Won't (Not)
Hold your hand in a fist with the thumb extended. Touch the thumb to your chin and then move your thumb forward while shaking your head from side to side.

Perish (Die)
Hold the right palm up and the left palm down. Turn both hands over so that the right palm is down and the left palm is up.

Eternal (Forever)
Hold up your right index finger and circle it in the air. Then bring your hand down and out with the thumb and little finger straight out. The three middle fingers are curled into the palm.

Life
Hold both hands at your waist with your thumbs and index fingers pointing out. Move the hands up along your chest.

Sign and Say

The community of believers was one in heart and mind.

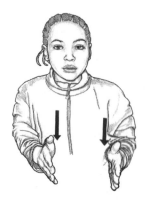

Community
Hold both hands open with fingers together. Touch the fingertips of both hands together as if you were making a roof. Twist your hands as you move them to the right.

Believers
Touch your forehead with the index finger of your right hand. Bring your hand down, palm flat, to meet your left hand, palm up. Clasp your hands together.

Believers *continued*
Hold your hands open with the palms facing each other in front of your body. Move both hands down in a parallel motion.

One
Hold up your index finger.

Heart
Use the second finger on each hand to outline the shape of a heart over the position of your actual heart.

Mind
Tap your index finger to your forehead twice.

Sign and Say

Acts 16:31

Believe in the Lord Jesus, and you will be saved.

Believe
Touch your forehead with
the index finger of your right
hand. Bring your hand down,
palm flat, to meet your left
hand, palm up. Clasp your
hands together.

Jesus
Touch the middle finger of
your right hand to the palm of
the left hand. Reverse.

You
Point away from yourself.

Saved
Hold your hands in fists and
cross them at the wrists, with
your palms facing your body.
Uncross your hands and turn
your fists so your palms face
away from your body.

Sign and Say

Romans 12:10

Love each other like the members of your family.

Love
Cross your fists at the wrists and press them to your heart.

Other
Hold your hand in a fist with thumb sticking out and palm down. Turn your hand over so that the palm is facing up.

Like (Same)
Hold your hand with your thumb and little finger out and your first three fingers curled down. Your palm faces down. Move your hand from side to side.

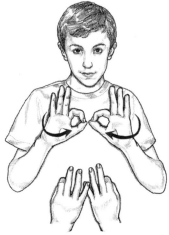
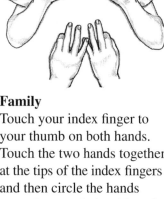

Family
Touch your index finger to your thumb on both hands. Touch the two hands together at the tips of the index fingers and then circle the hands around to touch the sides of the little fingers together.

Sign and Say

1 Corinthians 13:4

Love is patient, love is kind.

Love
Cross your fists at the wrists and press them to your heart.

Patient
Hold your right hand in a fist with the thumb out. Draw the thumb in a line from your mouth to your chin.

Kind
Hold your hands flat with palms touching and the right hand on top. Slide your right hand off your left.

Love never fails.

Love
Cross your fists at the wrists and press them to your heart.

Never
Hold your right hand near your left shoulder, with your palm facing to the left, and then wiggle the hand down.

Fails
Hold your left hand palm up. Hold your right hand with your thumb between your index finger and your second finger. Move your thumb and fingers across your left palm.

   Sign and Say

1 Corinthians 13:13

*Now faith, hope, and love remain—these three things—
and the greatest of these is love.*

Faith
Touch your right index finger to your forehead. Bring down your right hand, touching the tip of your index finger to the tip of your thumb to form a circle. Bring your left hand up with the index finger and thumb forming a second circle. Tap the two circles together.

Hope
Hold both hands with your palms open, facing the sides of your head. Your right hand should be above your head. Your left hand should be at eye level. Moving both hands at the same time, bend your hands to make a right angle with your fingers and then unbend them so that the fingers point straight up.

Love
Cross your fists at the wrists and press them to your heart.

Remain (Stay)
Hold out both hands with the little fingers and thumbs extended. Move your hands down in a short movement and hold them in place briefly.

Three
Hold up the thumb and first two fingers of your hand.

Greatest
Raise both hands up head high with palms facing out. Push hands slightly forward. Then bring hands down to shoulder level and push hands slightly forward again.

Love
Cross your fists at the wrists and press them to your heart.

Philippians 4:13

I can endure all these things through the power of the one who gives me strength.

I (Me)
Point to yourself.

Endure
Hold your right hand in a fist with your thumb out. Touch your thumb to the side of your nose and then wiggle it down in a line across your mouth to your chin.

All
Hold the left palm toward the body. Circle the right hand out and around the left palm. End with the back of the right hand in the open left hand.

Things
Hold your left hand palm up. Touch the back of your right hand to your left palm. Then bounce your right hand off the left hand to the right side.

Power
Bring both fists up in front of your left shoulder and move them to the right in front of your body.

One
Hold up your index finger.

Sign and Say

Gives
Hold both hands in front of
your body, palms up and
fingers and thumb touching on
each hand. Move your hands
up and away from your chest.

Me
Point to yourself.

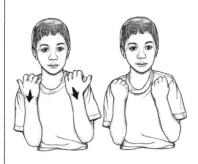

Strength (Courage)
Hold both hands with your
palms facing your shoulders
and your fingers spread apart.
Bring both hands forward as
you close both hands into fists
with the thumbs on the outside.

Dear friends, let's love each other, because love is from God.

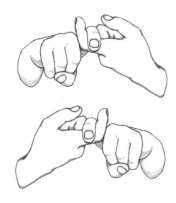

Friends
Hold out both hands with index fingers extended. Hook your right index finger over the left index finger. Reverse.

Love
Cross your fists at the wrists and press them to your heart.

Others
Hold your hand in a fist with thumb sticking out and palm down. Turn your hand over so that the palm is facing up.

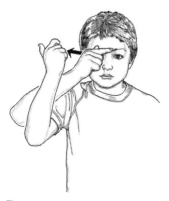

Because
Hold out the thumb and index finger on your right hand. Touch the tip of your index finger to your forehead and then quickly curl the finger back into your fist.

Love
Cross your fists at the wrists and press them to your heart.

God
Point the index finger of your right hand, with the other fingers curled down. Bring the hand down as if drawing a shepherd's crook while opening the palm.

Sign and Say

We love because God first loved us.

We
Hold up your index finger. Touch your right shoulder with the finger. Circle the finger out and touch it to your left shoulder.

Love
Cross your fists at the wrists and press them to your heart.

Because
Hold out the thumb and index finger on your right hand. Touch the tip of your index finger to your forehead and then quickly curl the finger back into your fist.

God
Point the index finger of your right hand, with the other fingers curled down. Bring the hand down as if drawing a shepherd's crook while opening the palm.

First
Touch the index finger of your right hand to the thumb of your left hand and raise both hands slightly.

Love
Cross your fists at the wrists and press them to your heart.

Us
Hold up the first two fingers of your right hand, pressing the other fingers down with the thumb. Touch your right shoulder with this hand. Circle your hand out and touch the fingers to your left shoulder.

Sign and Say

INDEX

Sign and Say